KB200580

감사와 공감

Thanks and Empathy

감사와 공감

지은이 | 이원로
초판 발행 | 2020. 8. 26
등록번호 | 제1988-000080호
등록된 곳 | 서울특별시 용산구 서빙고로65길 38
발행처 | 사단법인 두란노서원
영업부 | 2078-3352   FAX | 080-749-3705
출판부 | 2078-3331

책값은 뒤표지에 있습니다.
ISBN 978-89-531-3843-8 03230

독자의 의견을 기다립니다.
tpress@duranno.com   www.duranno.com

두란노서원은 바울 사도가 3차 전도여행 때 에베소에서 성령 받은 제자들을 따로 세워 하나님의 말씀으로 양육
하던 장소입니다. 사도행전 19장 8~20절의 정신에 따라 첫째 목회자를 돕는 사역과 평신도를 훈련시키는 사역,
둘째 세계선교(TIM)와 문서선교 (단행본·잡지) 사역, 셋째 예수문화 및 경배와 찬양 사역, 그리고 가정·상담 사역 등을
감당하고 있습니다. 1980년 12월 22일에 창립된 두란노서원은 주님 오실 때까지 이 사역들을 계속할 것입니다.

감사와 공감
Thanks and Empathy

이원로 8번째 한영대역 시선집
Lee Won-Ro's 8th Selected Poems

이원로 지음
Lee Won-Ro

Contents 목차

Part 2 제2부

Rehearsal 리허설

Part 3 제3부

Prelude to a Pilgrimage 장도壯途의 서막

Part 4 제4부

Daybreak 새벽

Part 5 제5부

Focal Point 초점

Thanks and Empathy

I look over for the beckon
And listen attentively to the call.

Aspire expecting to receive,
Cry hoping to be open.

Prayer washes away sorrow
While love clears away fear.

When empathy brings peace,
Thanks make dreams come true.

감사와 공감

손짓하기에 넘어다보고
부르기에 귀 기울이지

받게 되리니 열망하고
열어 주리니 울부짖지

기원이 슬픔을 씻어 내니
사랑은 두려움을 걷어 주지

공감이 화평을 가져오니
감사는 꿈을 이루게 하지

Part 1

Eve Celebration

전야제

A Cross Section

How do we know the whole only looking at a cross section?
Having long seen rather leads us to make a wrong guess;
We cannot recognize the whole with instant images
And a hasty conclusion shouldn't be made only by seeing
As a genuine value might not be perceived entirely.

Unexpected is coming on a sudden as this!
As not being properly prepared for,
Leaves and twigs are wildly blown off.
Without a moment to shore up the trunk,
Roots are pulled up by a rainstorm.

As the pulse reels off here,
Heart will begin to beat beyond.
Seemingly respiration subsides there
But the breath will rise again;
Appearing to be buried but soars up there.

단면

단면만 보고 어찌 전체를 알리
오래 보고도 자주 헛짚게 되지
찰나의 영상으론 전체를 모르지
보는 것만으로 속단할 수 없지
진정 값진 것은 다 안 보이기에

이렇게 갑자기 닥칠 줄이야
제대로 준비도 못 하였는데
잎과 가지가 마구 날려 간다
줄기를 지탱할 겨를도 없이
뿌리가 비바람에 뽑혀 간다

여기서 맥박이 풀려 가는 듯
너머서 다시 박동이 시작되지
호흡이 꺼져 가는 듯 저기서
다시 숨결이 피어 나오지
묻히는 듯 거기서 솟아오르지

A Living Promise

Are you dreaming?

What dream do you dream?

Anytime and anywhere,

The dream will come true.

Without cherishing a dream

How can you live even for a day!

You were born as such

Since your dream is your nourishment.

Though the day you accomplish it is far away,

A genuine dream must come true

As it is a living promise

Given to the earnest hope.

살아 있는 약속

꿈을 꾸는가
무슨 꿈을 꾸나
언제일지 어디서일지
이루어질 꿈이리

꿈을 먹지 않고 어찌
하루라도 살아가리
그토록 태어났지
꿈이 삶의 양식이기에

이루어질 날 아득해도
진정한 꿈은 성취되지
간절한 소망에 주어진
살아 있는 약속이기에

Infinite Exploration

A kite is flown high up
Beyond the eye's reach.
On a tight string to pass there,
It will soar endlessly.

Over the open door,
Passing the place unfolding
And following the shining star,
It goes into infinitely.

It flies into the deep space
Beyond the imagination's limit.
Grasping the signal to pass there
An infinite exploration will begin.

무한 탐사

연을 높이 띄워 올린다
눈길이 닿는 너머로
줄을 타고 거기를 지나
끝없이 올라가지

열리는 문 너머로
펼쳐지는 거기를 지나
눈부신 별을 따라
한없이 들어가지

심우주로 날아 들어간다
상상이 이르는 너머로
신호를 잡고 거기를 지나
무한 탐사가 시작되지

The Pursuit of Love

The day a biting wind blows,

Naked twigs tremble wildly,

But without any sign of fear

Perhaps as they get vitalized with the azure sky.

It's the time the will conquers the suffering.

A burly wood surrounds all directions.

Above is not seen covered with boughs,

Below is no way tangled with thornbushes,

I am fidgety being caught in fear.

It's the moment the hope of salvation arises.

I dash to the sole star

And rotate the untrodden orbit numerously,

Sometimes locked up solitary in the pitch dark.

Even driven into crisis, I show no sign of agitation

As the pursuit of love lulls panic.

사랑의 추구

칼바람이 불어치는 날
벌거벗은 가지가 마구 떨린다
웬일인지 두려운 기색이 없다
하늘빛이 좋아 기가 살아서리
의지가 고통을 이기는 때리

우람한 숲이 사방을 둘러쳤다
위는 가지에 가려 보이지 않고
아래는 가시가 엉켜 길이 없다
두려움에 잡혀 안절부절못한다
구원의 소망이 돋아나는 때리

유일한 별을 향하여 달려간다
전인미답의 궤도를 수없이 돈다
칠흑의 어둠에 홀로 갇히기도 하지
위기에 몰려도 동요의 기색이 없다
사랑의 추구가 공포를 잠재우는 때리

Windows of Revelation

The thing our senses can't grasp

By what will we perceive?

The place our perception can't reach

How will we approach to enter?

All the spheres our perception seizes,

All the things our senses touch,

Are windows of revelation extended from beyond.

Anytime and anywhere through these windows,

Endless messages will be sent.

As the windows of revelation are open all the time,

The day the fog clears with the wind,

An earnest eye can see at last

And enjoy a great pleasure holding the yonder side.

계시의 창

감각이 못 미치는 것은
무엇으로 알아차리게 되나
지각이 닿지 못하는 곳은
어떻게 다가가 들어서나

지각으로 파악되는 전 영역
감각이 닿는 세계의 모두는
너머서 내민 계시의 창들이리
언제나 어디서나 이 창으로
끊임없이 메시지를 보내오리

계시의 창은 늘 열려 있기에
바람이 불어 안개가 걷히는 날
간절한 눈은 드디어 보게 되리
너머를 잡는 큰 기쁨을 맛보리

An Esoteric Scroll

I do so
As I am willing to do.
But in fact
I will do
As I am told to do.

According to the words written by DNA
On an esoteric scroll,
Gathering materials and accumulating energy,
Flesh, mind and spirit grow out
To reveal the wondrous will.

By planting the functions of the infinite
In the finite
To help a creation,
Restlessly and ceaselessly,
Let me throw my heart and soul.

신비로운 두루마리

그렇게 하려 하여
그렇게 하지만
실은
그렇게 하라니
그렇게 하리

신비로운 두루마리에
DNA로 쓰여진 낱말대로
물질을 모으고 에너지를 쌓아
몸과 마음, 심령을 돋아 내리
놀라운 뜻을 드러내려서리

무한의 가능을
유한에 심어 주어
이루어 가도록
쉼 없이 끝없이
심혈을 토하게 하리

The Homing Instinct

Since when

And why, thither,

Growing longing

Deepens and deepens

In distress

And loneliness.

Invisible,

Inaudible,

But irresistible attraction

Makes us dash thither.

A country of earnest love

A rising aspiration will greet

And we can devote everything to and depend on.

Anytime and anywhere

Ceaselessly to spring up within,

A yearning has been

Planted deep in the soul.

Arrives even not having visited before

The homing instinct.

귀소본능

언제부터인지
왜인지 거기로
피어나는 그리움
괴로울 때
외로울수록
더욱 짙어 가지

보이지 않으나
들리지 않으나
떨칠 수 없는 끌림이
거기로 달려가게 하리
복받치는 열망이 맞을
모두를 맡기고 의지할
지극한 사랑의 나라지

어느 때나 어디서나
그침 없이 그 안으로
동경이 솟아오르게
심령 깊이 심어졌지
가본 적 없이도 도달하는
귀소본능이지

Ways and Dreams

Everyone alive

Has ways and dreams;

The given ways and

Blooming dreams.

To guard what is given

And adorn more magnificently,

The ways and dreams throughout our lives

Wrestle and dance.

The one will be delighted at

Having the route of longing

Combined with the orbit of predestination.

The other who goes astray will feel tormented.

길과 꿈

살아 있는 모두에는
길과 꿈이 있지
주어진 길과
피어나는 꿈

주어진 걸 지키려
보다 멋지게 꾸미려
길과 꿈은 한평생
씨름하며 춤추지

동경의 진로가
예정의 궤도와
함께 가는 이 신명 나리
엇가는 이 마음 아프지

My Song, My Dance

My song is my dream,

My life blooming to eternity

Will reach the infinitude in lush vines.

(As a deceit is uncovered,

Free from the dark,

Now I understand

All the world is

An amazing song.)

My dance is my hope,

Love waves flowing into perpetuity

Will form an infinitude ceaselessly billowing.

(Shedding fear

By defeating an evil spirit,

The whole universe is

An elaborate dance.

Now I can perceive.)

나의 노래 나의 춤

나의 노래는 나의 꿈
영원으로 피어오르는 나의 생명
무성하게 덩굴지어 무궁에 이르지
(거짓이 벗겨지며

어둠에서 풀려나니

천지가 모두

놀라운 노래인 걸

이제야 알게 되네)

나의 춤은 나의 소망
영겁으로 흘러드는 사랑의 물결
그침 없이 굽이치어 무한을 이루지
(악령을 물리치고

두려움을 떨치니

우주가 전부

정교한 춤인 걸

이제야 보게 되네)

The Gate of Truth

After having a dream,
The heart palpitates
In wonder and rapture
Because of the sound
As the heaven's gate opens.

The conductor remains
With his hand raised
At a concert hall after a grand finale.
Amid the profound resonance lingering,
The gate of truth will open.

How great the grace of God is shown
To the one for whom the gate opens!
A greater blessing is given
To the one who lives there
For so long and long.

진리의 문

꿈을 꾸고 나서
설레는 가슴은
하늘 문이
열리는 소리에
놀라고 황홀해서이리

지휘자가 손을
올린 채 멈추었다
대단원의 막이 내린 연주회장
심오한 여운 가운데
진리의 문이 열리리

얼마나 큰 은총인가
문이 열려진 이
더욱 큰 축복이지
아주 오래오래
그 안에 사는 이

An Eternal Nation

What is seen was

Not made out of what was visible*

What we do not see

Will rule what is seen.

Even looking at a distance,

He was delighted at the promise

And devoted everything to,

So he had received an eternal nation.

Being certain of

What we do not see*

And sure of

What we hope for.*

*Hebrews 11: 1-3

영원한 나라

보이는 것은 모두
안 보이는 데서 왔기에*
안 보이는 것이
보이는 것을 다스리지

먼발치서 바라보고도
약속을 기뻐했기에
모두를 들어 바쳤기에
영원한 나라를 받았지

안 보이는 것의
증거*를 보아서리
바라는 것의
실체*를 잡아서리
*히브리서 11:1-3

Somebody Might Pray

Not only the wind blows

But the clouds also scatter around.

Under the wondrous heaven,

The waves of hues billow.

Somebody might so pray;

Somebody might so permit.

Spring rain drizzles in the arid heart.

Flowers bloom in the dreary soul.

To the site where I sat up in fear at night

Affectionate tomorrow comes and embraces me.

Somebody might have implored anxiously,

So somebody might have responded to.

The day that seemed never to come

Mysteriously breaks and approaches.

The pang that seemed not to shed away

Clearly vanishes and submerges in peace.

Somebody might have wished wholeheartedly;

Somebody might have baptized for consolation.

누군가 기원했으리

바람만 불어오나
구름도 흩어지지
경탄할 하늘 아래
빛깔의 파도가 굽이친다
누군가 그리 기원했으리
누군가 그리 허락했으리

메마른 가슴에 봄비가 내린다
삭막한 영혼에 꽃이 피어난다
두려워 떨며 지새던 밤의 자리로
다정한 내일이 들어와 보듬어 준다
누군가 애타게 애원하였지
누군가 그래서 화답해 주었지

결코 올 것 같지 않던 날이
불가사의하게 열려 다가온다
떨칠 수 없을 것 같던 아픔이
씻은 듯 사라지고 평화에 잠긴다
누군가 마음 다해 기원하였지
누군가 위로의 세례를 내려 주었지

A Blinking Signal

Can you see the blinking dance of genes?
You may hear the sobbing sound flowing from the inside.

A crushing ceremony of stars are being held;
The soothing touch hidden may be noticed.

In a ball where a blinking signal rotates,
Waves of pity and pang undulate all the time.

The light will be turned off here
To celebrate an achievement sad but splendid.

And the light switched on there
To start a fabulous festival of welcome.

명멸 신호

유전자들의 명멸하는 춤을 보느냐
안에서 흘러오는 흐느낌도 들리리

별들의 참담한 의식이 열린다
숨어 쓰다듬는 손길도 보이리

명멸 신호가 회전하는 무도회에서는
아쉬움과 아픔의 물결이 늘 요동치지

불을 끄리 여기서
슬프나 아름다운 성취를 자축하며

불을 켜리 거기서
놀라운 환영의 축제를 시작하려

Trials and Errors

Life is a sea of aspiration,

Waves of timeless trials,

A tide of numerous errors,

A mystery spread out

According to an amazing plan

Of unknown from above.

To defeat death

Longing for eternity,

Endless trials have been made.

Will which arrow

Amid trials and errors

Hit the bull's eye?

Between light and dark,

Joy and sorrow,

We will live wrestling and dancing.

Why is a history of the earth to be written

As a process of trials and errors

Painful and pathetic?

시행착오

삶은 열망의 바다
무한한 시행의 파도
수많은 착오의 물결
위에서 내리는 알 수 없는
놀라운 계획에 따라
펼쳐지는 불가사의

영원이 그리워
죽음을 죽이려
끝없는 시도를 하리
어느 화살이
시행착오 가운데
급소에 적중될까

빛과 어둠 사이에서
기쁨과 슬픔 가운데서
씨름하며 춤추며 살지
어찌 아프고 안타까운
시행착오의 과정으로
땅의 역사를 쓰게 하나

Will and Plan

Not to be blighted before blooming,

Not to be scattered amid groaning,

We entreat with all our heart and soul.

Are we afraid of being rejected

And fearful of disappointing?

How time turns the wheel

Without any will?

Do we feel pity for

Fading hues?

Do we sigh for

Falling petals?

How the temporal whirl

Deprives beauty

Without any plan?

뜻과 계획

피기도 전에 시들지 않도록
신음 가운데 흩어지지 않게
마음과 심령 다해 애원하지
거절을 당할까 봐 두려운가
실망이 안겨질까 무서운가
어찌 아무 뜻도 없이
시간이 바퀴를 돌려 가리

안타까워하나
시들어 가는 빛깔을
한숨을 짓나
떨어지는 꽃잎에
어찌 아무 계획도 없이
시간의 회오리로
아름다움을 앗아가랴

Grafting

Not feeling
But you extend your hands to touch,
Put all your heart and soul
To become one by grafting.

To float stars
And bloom flowers,
You fly into
The place unseen.

Grafting means yearning
And prayer.
Believing you will be attached to,
You devote your whole life to.

접목

만져지지 않아도
닿으려 손을 내민다
마음과 혼을 다하리
접목되어 하나되려고

별을 띄우려
꽃을 피우려
안 보이는 데로
날아 들어가지

접목은 동경
접목은 기원
붙여 줄 줄로 믿고
모두를 맡기지

Part 2

Rehearsal

리허설

Rehearsal

Entering deep inside, where will you stand?

Ascending high up, what will you look at?

Being out through numerous rehearsals,

Where and what will you try to seize?

I stand on the horizon of deep space

And ride on the rolling gravity waves

To dedicate a magnificent concert

That will reach the origin of light.

A rehearsal is an endless wrestling,

A journey dashing to perfection,

And a course to achieve a victory

Erasing tenacious affection and arrogance.

리허설

깊이 들어가 어디에 서려나
높이 올라 무얼 내다보려나
무수한 리허설을 거쳐 나가
어디서 무엇을 잡으려는가

심우주의 지평에 서서
출렁이는 중력파를 타고
빛의 원천에 이르게 될
장엄한 연주를 바치려서리

리허설은 끊임없는 씨름
완전을 향해 달려가는 여정
끈덕진 애착과 교만을 지우며
승리를 이루어 가는 과정

A Wondrous Echo

Will be blown away with the wind
The breath of lamentation.
Will be blown in with the wind
The vibration of wonder.

Always from a site
Invisible and inaudible
The wind blows in and away
Scattering here by reverberation
The ecstasy of the place.
Caressing by the merciful hand
To strip here off the sorrow.

The wind blows in all the time
To send a wondrous echo
The wind blows out endlessly
To take sadness and ache away.

경이로운 울림

바람에 불려 가리
비탄의 숨소리
바람에 불려 오리
경이로운 울림

안 보이고 안 들리는
모르는 데서 늘
바람이 불어오고 가지
그곳 환희를 여기에
울림으로 뿌려 주리
자비의 손으로 어루만져
이곳 비애를 벗겨 가리

바람은 언제나 불어온다
경이로운 울림을 전하려
바람이 한없이 불어 간다
슬픔과 아픔을 벗겨 가려

Tapping Sound

On hearing a tapping sound,
Opening the door as I greet,
Dark clouds are scattered
And a shining sky in my sight.

Amazing ability
Tugs at my heartstrings
To caress the deep inside,
So I will not be shaken.

As the head beholds
And the heart expects,
I may have known who is making
The tapping sound.

Greeting with joy
Makes me attain a mirthful country.
As I admire and long for,
I will live in the nation.

두드리는 소리

두드리는 소리에
문을 열어 맞이하니
먹구름이 흩어지며
눈부신 하늘이 들어온다

놀라운 능력이
심금을 울려 주고
깊은 속을 다져 주어
흔들리지 않았지

바라보는 머리이기에
고대하는 가슴이기에
두드리는 소리가
누구인지 알았지

기쁨으로 맞이하니
환희의 나라를 얻지
기리고 고대하기에
그 나라에서 살게 되리

Attraction

Between nucleus and electron,

Amid fixed stars and planets,

Attraction not dispellable

Will turn into circulating longing.

The heart that can't let go for being lonely,

The soul that can't leave for being afraid,

The zealotry devoting everything for being pining for,

All the world gets involved in the history of attraction.

As there is attraction,

The world is created.

Life means

An endless itinerary of attraction.

Attraction is entreaty,

Entreaty is permission,

Permission is dedication,

And dedication is predestination.

끌림

핵과 전자 사이
항성과 행성 가운데
떨칠 수 없는 끌림이
선회하는 그리움이 되리

외로워 잡고 못 놓는 마음
두려워 품고 못 뜨는 심령
그리워 모두를 바치는 열망
세상은 모두 끌림의 역사이리

끌림이 있기에
세상이 생겼지
삶은 끌림의
끝없는 여정이지

끌림은 간청
간청은 허용
허용은 드림
드림은 예정

The Nation of Light

The day when May blooms,
With the wind clearing clouds
Under the fine open sky
Green waves are bright.

Riding on the numerous dancing photons
Sprinkled over the glossy leaves,
I enter the wondrous nation of light unseen
As it is hidden with worldly dust.

Not fallen down withered
But newly blooming country of lives everyday,
The nation of light is not buried in darkness.
All is shown to be the window of revelation.

빛의 나라

오월이 피어나는 날
바람은 구름을 걷고
맑게 열린 하늘 아래
초록의 파도가 눈부시다

윤기 나는 잎새 위에 뿌려지는
무수한 광자들의 무도에 실려
세상 먼지에 가려서 안 보이던
경이로운 빛의 나라로 들어간다

시들어 떨어져 버리는 게 아니라
매일 새로 피어나는 삶의 나라지
어둠에 묻히지 않는 빛의 나라지
보여주는 모두는 계시의 창이지

Farewell

A rainstorm with rough thunder and lightning

Has made the observing heart to stew,

Then at last the thin string cut off

To cause the blood stop circulating through the worn-out

body.

A waned, wasted and worn figure

That once contained the blooming season

Turns into its origin with 90-minute baptism of fire.

The bowlful ash fills the jar.

Agony, apprehension, grief and death

All were clearly burned out.

An azure sky of autumn even in the rainy spell

Soothes the procession of parting.

Here the farewell is over now,

There a welcome ceremony will begin.

환송

천둥 번개 요란한 비바람이
지켜보는 가슴을 졸이더니
가느다란 줄이 드디어 끊겨
지친 몸에 피 돌기가 그친다

꽃피던 시절을 한때 담았던
시들고 깡마른 초췌한 모습
불세례 90분에 본시로 가지
한 사발 재로 단지에 담긴다
아픔과 두려움 슬픔과 죽음도
모두 말끔히 태워 버렸으리

장마 중인데 가을 하늘을 내려
환송 행렬을 두루 어루만져 준다
여기서 이제 환송이 끝났으니
거기서 환영 행사가 시작되지

Brief Grief

Luxuriant verdure undulates
On the boughs where petals blown away.

Always behind the eyes of the end,
The smile of the beginning is hidden.

Wherever end and beginning exist,
Ceremonies of meeting and parting will happen.

After the brief grief ends,
An extended exultation will soon start.

짧은 슬픔

꽃잎이 날려 간 가지에서
무성한 초록이 물결친다

끝의 눈빛들 뒤에는 늘
시작의 미소가 숨어 있지

끝과 시작이 있는 곳에는 어디나
만남과 헤어짐의 예식이 있지

짧은 슬픔이 끝난 다음
긴 기쁨이 곧 시작되지

Ten Millennia and Myriad Years

The sound brought over the deep space;
The oscillation shaking the heart;
Do you know who makes the sound?
Amid the dances of dispersing nebulae
The passing sound of ten millennia and myriad years.

Glimmering groups
Lined on the horizon of the brain;
Do you know who are going to do what?
The flock of camels are fighting to practice
Passing the eye of a needle.

만년 억년

심우주 너머서 오는 소리
심장을 흔들어 대는 진동
누가 내는 소리인지 아는가
흩어지는 성운들의 무도 가운데
만년 억년이 스쳐 가는 소리지

뇌의 지평에 늘어선
아물거리는 무리들
누가 무얼 하려는지 아나
낙타의 무리들이 다투어
바늘구멍 지나가는 연습 중이지

Wings and Legs

With thick thighs, you can reign over the land.
Flying high up, you can go to dreamland.

It seems all right only to have wings,
But even flying birds have legs.

The greater the wings are, the more ornamental the legs;
The thicker the legs are, the more imitative the wings.

To live on the land, big legs are suitable
But to fly over the sky, they are hard to handle.

What you want is greater wings and decorative legs
Or thicker legs and imitative wings.

날개와 다리

다리가 굵어야 땅에 군림하지
높이 날아야 꿈나라에 이르지

날개만 있어도 될 듯싶은데
나는 새도 다리가 달려 있다

날개가 클수록 다리는 시늉만 있고
다리가 클수록 날개는 흉내만 냈다

땅에 살기에는 큰 다리가 십상이지
하늘을 날려면 큰 다리는 주체스럽지

바라는 게 큰 날개에 시늉 다리인가
원하는 게 큰 다리에 흉내 날개인가

The One Who Pays Attention to

The heart heats hot
To ignite thinking.
The light flits
To let the soul swing.
The one who holds and yields fruit
Is a real blessing.

The light glitters all the time
And waves its hands everywhere.
The chance will be given only to
The one who pays attention to.
Amid emotional tears,
He will taste awakening.

기울이는 이

마음이 뜨거워지며
생각에 불이 인다
빛이 스쳐 지나가며
심령이 흔들리리
붙들어 열매 맺는 이
진정 축복이어라

빛은 늘 번득이고
어디서나 손짓하는데
기울여 쏟는 이에게만
기회가 주어지지
감동의 눈물 가운데
깨달음을 맛보리

The Last Enemy

Who can escape Death's authority?
Nobody possibly gets off its hands
For Death as the fount of all agonies and grieves
Would create a great sea of transience of life.

An uncalled-for guest you feel fearful and hateful
Will not drop out like a shadow clinging to.
Regardless of being terrified or indifferent,
All will be snatched away when time is due.

Nobody knows the day and the moment
Being brave on the surface but apprehensive inside.
You and I will live on trembling within it;
You and I will live with tears and smiles.

As it is written that "The last enemy
to be destroyed is death"*
We'll see the very day of victory
Amid the rapture at last as promised.*
1 Corinthians 15:26

마지막 원수

누가 죽음의 권세를 탈출하랴
아무도 그 손아귀를 못 벗어나지
모든 고뇌와 애수의 원천으로
인생무상의 큰 바다를 이루지

두려워하며 미워하는 불청객이나
그림자처럼 붙어 떨어지지 않지
겁에 질려도 무시해도 상관없이
때가 되면 가차 없이 채어 가리

그날과 그때는 아무도 모르기에
겉으로는 담대하나 속으론 겁내지
너와 나 그 안에서 떨며 살아가지
나와 너 거기서 울고 웃으며 살지

"멸망당할 마지막 원수는
죽음이다"* 하였으니
이미 받은 승리의 그날을
드디어 환희 가운데 보리
*고린도전서 15:26

Your Future and My Future

Your music

And my painting

Are just our future.

Do we hesitate and doubt

Or are we confident and daring?

What shall we grasp?

Your dance and my song,

My stage and your performance

Will be our future.

Not too loudly

But dauntlessly,

We will paint our way to go.

너와 나의 미래

너의 음악
나의 그림이
너와 나의 미래지
주저하고 의심하느냐
자신 있고 담대한가
무엇을 잡으려는가

너의 춤 나의 노래
나의 무대 너의 연주가
너와 나의 미래지
너무 요란하지 않게
그러나 담대하게
가야 할 길을 색칠하리

Vibration and Trembling

The progress of the mind
Will be known by the color overlaid.
Amid the timbre recollected,
The prospect of the future will be seen.

Echoes of strange hues;
Vibrations of splendid instruments;
Immoderate impulse should be avoided
And excessive obsession is forbidden.

Thickness of the overlaid color
Will reveal the location to anchor.
Composition and tune of the recapitulation
Is the site where the soul stays.

울림과 떨림

덧칠해 가는 색깔로
마음의 흐름을 알리
되새기는 음색 가운데
장래의 전망이 보이리

기묘한 빛깔들의 울림
장려한 악기들의 떨림
지나친 충동은 피해야지
과다한 집착은 금물이리

되바르는 색깔의 짙기로
닻을 내릴 곳이 보이리
재현부의 구성과 음조가
영혼의 초점이 사는 데지

Wings of Tunes

For ages somewhere
Trapped and locked up,
At last they soar flapping.

With aspiring vibrations
And entreating reverberations,
Fluttering tunes
Between brightness and darkness
Are on the wings toward the zenith
By groping vicissitudes.

After having roamed with no name
Amid dust and din,
They sing crossing the firmament.

With ardent yells
And anxious moans,
The tenacious wings of tunes
Holding the rope from the Heaven
And drawn by the rays
Climb and climb.

선율의 날개

그동안 오래 어딘가
붙들려 갇혀 있더니
드디어 활개 쳐 솟는다

열망의 떨림으로
간구의 울림으로
퍼덕이는 선율
빛과 어둠 사이
우여곡절을 더듬으며
천정을 향해 날개 친다

먼지와 소음 가운데서
이름도 없이 방황하더니
창공을 가르며 노래한다

간절한 외침으로
애타는 하소연으로
매달리는 선율의 날개
빛살이 그려 주는
천상의 줄을 잡고
오르고 또 올라간다

Expectation and Preparation

With the expectation,

The sun rises and the moon sets.

Amid the preparation,

Constellations rise and galaxies set.

A millennium flows out

And then eternity draws near.

As the preparation has been made,

Flowers fall and stars fade.

Up to the expectation,

Stars rise and flowers bloom.

Hardships pass

And joys draw near.

As there is expectation,

Our meeting will turn out delightful.

As there is preparation,

Our parting will not be pathetic.

Joyful as we get

But not hurt when we lose.

기대와 준비

기대 가운데
해가 뜨고 달이 지리
준비 가운데
성좌가 뜨고 은하가 지리
천년이 흘러가고
만년이 다가오지

준비가 되었기에
꽃은 떨어지고 별은 지지
기대에 맞추어
별이 뜨고 꽃이 피리
고난은 지나가고
환희가 다가오지

기대가 있기에
만남이 기쁘게 되리
준비가 있기에
이별이 서럽지 않지
얻으니 기쁘고
잃어도 안 아프지

Heaven's Gate

With a bow lifted high and tugged deep,

With the keyboard pressed nimbly,

With the heart composed and the breath blown to the
fullest

By the tremor of tunes

And the vibration of hues,

A nation of wonder wide and wide

A country of mystery lofty and lofty

We grope the windows and doors

And tap ceaselessly.

The trembling timbre tapped

And the stream of tones stroked

Raise a wondrous wind

And create preternatural clouds

To open the Heaven's Gate in a flash

With the roll of thunder

And the rays of lightning.

Every instant on the Earth

Will last eternally in ecstasy.

하늘 문

활을 높이 들어 깊이 그어
건반을 민첩히 두드려
가슴을 다듬어 입김을 다하여
음률의 떨림으로
색깔의 울림으로
넓고 넓은 경이의 나라
높고 높은 신비의 왕국
창과 문을 더듬어 댄다
그침 없이 두드려 댄다

두드려 내는 음색의 울림이
문질러 내는 음정의 흐름이
경이로운 바람을 일으켜
신비로운 구름을 띄워
천둥이 울려 주는 소리로
번개가 비쳐 주는 빛깔로
하늘 문을 홀연 열어 주리
땅에서 살아가는 순간들이
황홀 안에 영원히 살게 되리

Part 3

Prelude to a Pilgrimage

장도壯途의 서막

Order

Life is a duty of worship,

The duty means a life of devotions.

We will live working,

Worshiping through duty.

A truthful life is divine service.

If an order between above and below breaks,

The relationship of neighbors will also collapse.

As fame turns into idolatry

Adoring popular applause,

A guilty conscience and void will ensue.

The start stands straight,

Then, all will recover.

The objects of comparison will be missing

And the green-eyed monster and conflict will vanish,

Just superbness and sincerity will remain.

질서

삶은 섬기는 일
일은 예배하는 삶
일하며 살아가리
일을 통해 섬기고
진실한 삶이 예배이리

위아래 질서가 깨지면
이웃 관계도 무너지지
명성이 우상이 되니
갈채를 섬기게 되리
자책과 허무가 뒤따르리

처음이 바로 서면
모두가 회복되지
비교의 대상이 없어지고
시기와 다툼은 사라지리
탁월과 신실만 남게 되리

Still

No matter how we make a resolution,

We feel vacant in the heart.

Something is lost and lacking,

 We beat the chest looking out the distant hill.

Knowing but not working well,

We turn back and sigh in solitude.

Though we've received ages ago,

Still we spread our hand wistfully.

We have long been accustomed to accepting to live,

Still we live not knowing who the donor is.

Already the kingdom has been bequeathed,

Still unbelieving we wander the fields.

아직도

아무리 다짐을 해보아도
마음 한 구석이 허전하다
무언가 빠지고 부족해서
먼 산 바라보며 가슴 치리
알면서도 마음대로 안 되니
돌아서서 홀로 한숨짓지

이미 받은 지 오래되었는데
아직도 안타까이 손을 벌린다
받아먹고 사는 지 이미 오랜데
아직도 주는 이 모르고 살지
이미 왕국을 안겨 준 지 오랜데
아직도 못 믿고 벌판을 헤맨다

Transition Period

Temporal travel is

A continuum of infinite transitions

Between a spectacular prelude

And a solemn denouement.

As heart-scorching

Flames flared up,

Admirable hues

Might cover the world.

Our itinerary is

A sequence of incessant transitions

Between the message of morning glow

And the revelation of evening glow.

과도기

시간의 여정은
한없는 과도기의 연속
아름다운 서막과
장엄한 대단원 사이

가슴을 태우는
불길이 일기에
경탄할 빛깔로
세상을 덮지

우리의 여정은
끝없는 과도기의 연속
아침놀의 메시지와
저녁놀의 계시 사이

Day after Day

As earthly illustrations created with
Conceit and self-righteousness disappear,
An amazing world is wide open
Descending from on high.
Day after day is the day of glory,
Every day is the day of revelation.

As brilliant auspicious vitality
Defeats the darkness on the earth,
The moments that must fade away
Will anchor in eternity
Riding on the emotional wave
Flowing down from Heaven.

As the frightening night has drawn back
Submerged in scuffles and self-condemnations,
The thrill of ecstasy will be full
Spurting from the inmost heart.
Day after day is the day of triumph,
Every day is the day of blessing.

하루하루

자만과 독선이 이룬
땅의 삽화가 사라져 가니
가장 높은 데서 내려주는
놀라운 세계가 펼쳐진다
하루하루가 영광의 날
하루하루가 계시의 날

눈부신 아침의 서기가
땅의 어둠을 물리치니
하늘에서 흘러내리는
감동의 큰 물결을 타고
사라져야 할 순간들이
영원 안에 닻을 내리리

다툼과 자책에 잠긴
두려운 밤이 물러가니
가장 깊은 데서 솟아나는
환희의 떨림이 가득하지
하루하루가 승리의 날
하루하루가 축복의 날

Late Autumn

How elegant and extraordinary

Fleeting beauty is!

Amid enigma

The feature dimly emerges:

Dazzling hues and shining smile

Flower the time gained in full bloom.

Before blizzard comes

They will enjoy late autumn given.

The yearning glance will covertly

Run beyond the remote sea.

The vexing heart has now been

Embraced in the lofty heaven.

Running with no words for

Probably an amazing world that awaits.

Being hauled away without knowing

As the omnipotence has drawn.

What is frightening is not the sea of oblivion

But the road of time unmanageable.

How writhing can solve?

Only truth will tell us the time.

만추

우아하고 경이롭다
스쳐가는 아름다움
불가해한 가운데로
아스라이 드는 모습
눈부신 색깔 빛나는 미소
언은 때를 활짝 피어 낸다
눈보라가 몰려오기 전에
주어진 만추를 만끽하리

동경의 눈길은 남몰래
먼 바다 너머를 달리리
애타던 가슴은 이제
드높은 하늘에 안겼지

아무 말 없이 달려가는 길
놀라운 세상이 기다려선가
알지도 못하고 끌려가는 길
거역 못할 큰 힘이 당겨서리
두려운 건 망각의 바다보다도
헤아릴 수 없는 시간의 길이지
몸부림으로 어찌 해결되겠는가
진리가 오직 때를 알게 해주리

Night Lightning

As I woke up by a lightning
Thunderbolts shake the window panes
The rainstorm is blowing hard
To raise boisterous waves in night wood.

Upon the frightening call of flash
A soul startled from sleep
Riding on thunder and lightning
Soars up to the zenith.

Stripping of old clothing,
Flashes of lightning will put on new light.
Thunders tug the heartstrings
To sprout wings on the soul.

밤 번개

번갯불에 깨어나니
천둥이 창을 흔든다
불어치는 비바람이
밤 숲에 격랑을 인다

섬광의 놀라운 부름에
소스라쳐 눈뜬 영혼이
천둥과 번개에 올라타고
천정을 향해 솟구친다

헌 옷을 말끔히 벗기고
번개로 새 빛을 입히지
천둥으로 심금을 두드려
영혼에 날개를 돋아 내리

Silver Grass Hill

Slanted rays of light
Pour entirely down on the silver grass hill.
Riding on the flow of time
Silver grasses dance in full bloom.

Winds blow as you like
Blizzards rage as you wish
When your turn is over, my turn will come
I will endure prostrated flat
Even being broken, that's not an end.
Blown away, there will be a place to live in.

On the silver grass hill covered with the sunset glow
Magnificent music is resounding
First, a tune of farewell
Then that of adoration sinking into the sea.

억새 동산

기우는 빛살이 온통
억새 동산에 쏟아진다
시간의 흐름을 타고
억새 꽃 춤이 한창이다

바람아 불 테면 불어라
눈보라야 칠 테면 쳐라
네가 끝나면 내 차례가 오리
납작 엎드려 참고 버티지
부서진다고 어찌 끝이랴
날려 가도 어딘가에 가 살지

낙조에 잠긴 억새 동산에서
장려한 음악이 울려 퍼진다
처음엔 고별의 가락이더니
예찬의 선율로 바다에 잠긴다

Heavenly Smile

Hugging the heavenly pleasure
Sprinkled by the bright morning sun,
Where to behold with elegant eyes?

Shaking off the pain of a terrible night
Soaring flaps of wings,
Who gives that heavenly smile?

What dress is suitable to put on?
What dance is proper to sway?
How to sing to repay?

Tearing but not being sunk;
Sighing but not being bound;
Winning but not being enraptured.

천상의 미소

영롱한 아침 해로 뿌려 주는
하늘의 기쁨을 한 아름 안고
우아한 눈길 어디를 바라보나

끔찍한 밤의 아픔을 털고
날아오르는 날개의 활갯짓
천상의 미소는 누가 피우나

무슨 옷을 입어야 어울릴 건가
어떤 춤을 추어야 제격일 건가
어떻게 노래 불러 보답하려나

눈물짓나 거기에 침몰 않지
탄식하나 거기에 결박 안 되지
이기나 거기에 취하지 않지

Raining River

Riding on the raining river,
Our days flow.
On the bridge with rain scattering,
We meet an eternal love.

With invisible strings and beads,
Heaven holds the ground.
To remind the love from time immemorial,
Pouring water will cover hills and streams.

Not a meager mirth
Merely linked with thin threads,
But plentiful pleasure might have been entreated
And an endless win prayed.

Longing for an astonishing appearance of tomorrow,
Our river meanders its way.
On the day we defeat the final enemy,
We will go into the dazzling land of promise.

비 내리는 강

비 내리는 강을 타고
우리의 날은 흘러가고
빗발치는 다리 위에서
영원한 사랑을 만나지

안 보이는 줄과 구슬로
하늘이 땅을 늘 붙들더니
태초의 사랑을 일깨우려
물세례로 강산을 덮지

가는 실로 겨우 이어진
가냘픈 기쁨이 아니라
풍성한 환희를 간구했으리
끝없는 승리를 기원했으리

놀라울 내일의 모습을 그리며
우리의 강은 굽이쳐 흘러가지
마지막 원수를 이기게 될 날에
눈부실 약속의 땅에 들게 되리

Dusk

We cross the bridge at dusk
On our way out is one-way as on the way in.
The horizon still blazes with the glorious sunset glow,
Figures appearing over that scene.
At last, a new portal will be opened faintly.

Grasping a ray of light given,
We cross the bridge boldly.
With no shake but straight sight,
Not to be beguiled by a flock of crow
And not to lose our footing by lightning bolts.

At dusk we
Cross the bridge led by dreams.
A genuine dream is not a mirage
But the ark of the living covenant
Already recorded in the beginning.

땅거미

땅거미 내리는 다리를 건너간다
온 길처럼 가는 길도 일방통행로
지평은 아직 노을로 놀랍게 타고
그 너머로 피어 드러나는 형상들
드디어 새 문이 아스라이 열리지

주어진 한줄기 빛을 움켜쥐고
담대히 다리를 건너가야 하리
흔들림 없이 시선을 바로잡아
까마귀 떼에 현혹되지 않으시길
번갯불에 놀라 실족하지 마시길

땅거미 질 때 우리는
꿈에 이끌려 다리를 건너지
진정한 꿈은 신기루가 아니라
태초에 이미 기록된
살아 있는 언약의 본체이지

Morning Glow

Brilliant hues of morning glow
Reflected on the morning dew
Reveal the kingdom of heaven briefly
With patterns of the fading season.

The aisle light enters,
The profound will that leads us,
And the blindfolded mind's eye
All will be opened with due time.

Always staying there,
But He will let us see it just for a moment.
To anyone and anywhere,
It will be seen only when awake.

아침노을

아침이슬에 반사되는
영롱한 노을의 빛깔
기우는 계절을 무늬지어
하늘나라를 힐끗 드러낸다

빛이 들어오는 통로도
이끌어 가는 심오한 뜻도
가려졌던 마음의 눈도
때가 차야만 열려지리

언제나 거기에 있는데
오직 잠시만 보게 해주리
누구에게나 어디서나
눈이 열릴 때만 보이리

Resonance of Rays of Light

Plentiful photons dance
Burning over the horizon.
No way to comprehend by looking around
From where they come and to where they go.

By pouring a pack of photons over
Toward the core of chaotic darkness,
He has revealed majestic time and space
With wondrous resonance of rays of light.
Like dances of stars and songs of flowers,
Tremor of photons and humming of hues
Will go paint the world endlessly
And resonance of rays rule over time and space.

As the cosmic color changes
With the dances of photons,
The light resonance arising in the mind
Will form joys and sorrows of the world

빛의 공명

무수한 광자들의 무도가
지평을 태우며 넘어간다
어디서 와 어디로 가는지
둘러보아도 알 길 없다

혼돈의 암흑 가운데로
광자의 무리를 쏟아 날려
불가사의한 빛의 공명으로
장려한 시공을 드러낸다
별들의 춤, 꽃들의 노래처럼
광자의 떨림, 색깔의 울림이
세상을 끝없이 색칠해 가리
빛의 공명이 시공을 다스리지

광자들의 무도에 따라
우주 빛깔이 변해 가듯
마음에 이는 빛의 공명이
세상의 애환을 지어가리

Prayer

Brilliant waves flood in

From a faraway sea where the sun rises.

Your will

Be my wish;

And Your plan

Be my hope, I pray.

How should You admit impossibility yourself?

Bless us to achieve abundantly

By bestowing us Your wisdom, knowledge and power

And leading us to do our share of work properly.

Over the sea with the sun setting

Waves carry away the evening glow.

Amid Your joy,

My hope will anchor;

Amid Your glory,

My soul will settle safe, I pray.

기도

해 뜨는 먼 바다에서
눈부신 물결이 밀려온다
당신의 뜻이
나의 염원이 되게 하시고
당신의 계획이
나의 소망이 되게 하소서

당신에게 어찌 불가능이 있을까요
당신의 지혜와 지식과 능력을 주셔서
주신 일 잘 감당하게 인도하소서
넉넉히 이루도록 축복하여 주소서

해 지는 바다 너머로
파도가 낙조를 담아 간다
당신의 기쁨 가운데
나의 소망이 닻을 내리게 하소서
당신의 영광 가운데
나의 영혼이 안착하게 하소서

Mount Nebo

Forty years' glory in the royal court,

Forty years' suffering in exile,

And forty years' obedience in wilderness,

All were past pilgrimage.

Here, east of the Dead Sea,

The peak of Pisgah,

Mount Nebo, he climbed.

Not allowed to enter but far away

The future spreading the land of promise,

He saw with clear eye.

What a great grace!

From here only uphill roads

From now on no downhills

Infinite blessing!

Even at the height of suffering and sorrow,

As he kept the promise and followed,

He was led to the summit

To show as far as he could see

The place prohibited from entering

With the clothing of this side

And what will happen in the future.

느보산

궁중의 영화 40년
유형의 고난 40년
광야의 순종 40년
모두가 스쳐 간 순례 여정
여기 사해의 동쪽
비스가의 정상
느보산에 올랐다

들어갈 수 없으나 멀리서
약속의 땅 펼쳐질 미래를
맑은 눈으로 바라보았으니
어찌 큰 은혜 아닌가
여기부터 오르는 길만 있고
지금부터 내리막은 없으리니
한없는 축복이리

고통과 슬픔의 절정에서도
약속을 붙잡고 따랐기에
여기 옷 입고는
들어갈 수 없는 곳
장차 이루어질 일을
눈이 닿는 데까지 보여 주려
정상으로 이끌어 주었으리

Pupil

Deep and deeper, you and I

Look into pupils.

The upcoming future restlessly

Will dance with the remote past.

Solemn sounds shake the world

To expand the universe infinitely.

Within brain cells and fibers numerously entangled,

Emotive galaxies, intellectual constellations

And spiritual cosmoses will circle together.

My pupils

And your pupils,

But something enormous

Unimaginable before is in.

So much startled and awe-struck.

As I don't know,

That is not mine, certainly.

As you don't know, either,

That is not yours, surely.

눈동자

깊이 더 깊이 너와 나
눈동자를 들여다보자
밀려드는 미래가 쉼 없이
까마득한 옛날과 무도하리
장엄한 음악이 천지를 흔들며
한없이 우주를 팽창해 가리
수없이 얽힌 뇌세포와 섬유 속에
감성의 은하군 지성의 성좌들
영성의 우주들이 함께 선회하리

나의 눈동자인데
너의 눈동자인데
전에는 상상도 못하던
엄청난 게 들어 있다
너무나 놀랍고 두렵다
나도 모르니
내 것 아닌 게 분명하다
너도 모르니
네 것 아닌 것도 자명하다

Prelude to a Pilgrimage

Numerous maple leaves

Blown away by cold wind;

Migratory birds' dance

Leaving in a flock;

Amazing panorama is present

On the pouring rays of a setting sun.

No sign of fear at all,

But only wild yells are loud.

No sad expression is seen,

But joyful dances cover the world.

Doubting and wandering being stripped of,

Confident look is clear.

A thing flown away far-off

Is not the vanishing one to the last.

Along the wondrous itinerary,

A road flows to the next.

A denouement uncovered here

Is a prelude to a pilgrimage to open the other side.

장도의 서막

찬바람에 날려 가는
무수한 단풍잎들
떼를 지어 떠나는
철새들의 무도
쏟아지는 해넘이 빛살에
놀라운 파노라마를 연다

두려운 빛은 전혀 없다
열광의 외침만 요란하다
슬픈 기색은 보이지 않고
기쁜 춤이 천지를 덮는다
의심과 방황이 벗겨지며
확신의 눈빛이 완연하다

가마아득히 날려가는 건
끝내 사라지는 게 아니지
경이로운 여정을 따라서
다음으로 흘러드는 길이리
여기에서 펼쳐지는 대단원은
저쪽을 여는 장도의 서막이리

Part 4

Daybreak

새벽

Infinitude within Finitude

Apparent finitude on the surface,
But minutely examined within,
Infinitude flows hidden deep.

We grow graveled
And tremble hard by astonishment
At being reborn.

As the love of devotion kills Death,
Finitude enters infinitude by Faith.
A journey makes us become one in awe.

Finitude living in infinitude;
Infinitude surviving within finitude;
An authentic mystery of life.

유한 속 무한

겉보기는 분명 유한인데
안에 들어 자세히 살피니
무한이 깊숙이 숨어 흐른다

어리둥절해지지
놀라 마구 떨리지
다시 살아난다니

헌신의 사랑이 죽음을 죽여
유한이 믿음으로 무한에 드는
경이롭게 하나 되는 여정이지

무한 속에 사는 유한
유한 속에 사는 무한
진정 삶의 신비이다

The Flower of Yearning

The flower yearning blooms,

Coming from the loftiest,

Can hold the light of the home

And grow into an emblem of genuine love

With sound appearance and aroma.

Always at the crossroads of

Harmony and confrontation,

It will receive the way to go

By yelling

To the heaven.

As we devote all,

While glossing life with truth,

It will bloom the most beautiful flower

In the world that never wither

And sprinkle perfume of surprise.

동경의 꽃

동경이 피어 내는 꽃은
지고(至高)에서 왔기에
본고장의 빛을 담고 있지
온전한 모습과 향기로
참사랑의 표상이 되리

조화와 대결의
갈림길에서 늘
하늘을 우러러
부르짖어
갈 길을 받지

삶을 진실로 닦아 가며
모두를 들어 바치기에
세상에서 가장 아름다운
시들지 않을 꽃을 피우지
놀라운 향기를 뿌려 주리

The Eye of a Storm

Such a rough blizzard
Sweeping hills, streams and the sea,
What shall be done?
A mesocyclone flooding in
And the eye of a storm raging
Will remind us something.

As having constructed an impregnable fort,
You've boasted the solid mountain fortress.
Is it for someone to tap it to test?
A horrible scene and atrocious appearance
Raising the fear to the extremity
To measure the depth of love.

The eye of a storm anywhere is
Menacing and mighty capacity
To drive us to despair or awakening.
The scene of Armageddon*
Is carved deep by seeing it in advance
To let us know the producer.
*Revelation 16: 16

폭풍의 눈

이처럼 거센 눈보라로
산하와 바다를 휩쓰니
무얼 어찌 하려서인가
몰려드는 소용돌이 구름
휘몰아치는 폭풍의 눈으로
무언갈 깨우쳐 주려선가

난공불락의 요새를 지었다고
네가 자랑하는 견고한 산성을
누군가 두드려 보는 시험인가
처절한 광경 광포한 모습으로
두려움을 극대로 치켜 올려
사랑의 깊이를 재 보려서리

폭풍의 눈은 어디서나
위협적이고 강렬한 능력
절망케도 깨닫게도 하리
아마겟돈의 결전* 모습을
미리 보여 깊이 새겨 넣어
연출자를 알게 하려서리
*요한계시록 16:16

Absolute Silence

To the ultimate accomplishment,

The universe rushes infinitely.

From where the inexhaustible

Marvelous energy of Big Bang comes?

So enriched and further enriched

That no more hardening is seen possible

For the hottest particle

Within absolute silence.

The wondrous energy turning

Aspiration into achievement,

Where does it come from?

Within absolute silence

That leads to a miracle.

"You need only to be still."*

You will see the way revealed

With the sea split.

*Exodus 14:14

절대 침묵

궁극의 성취를 향하여
우주는 한없이 돌진하지
빅뱅의 무궁무진한
놀라운 에너지는 어디서 오나
농축되고 더욱 농축되어
더는 다질 수 없게 안 보이는
가장 뜨거운 알맹이
절대 침묵 속이리

열망을 성취로 이끄는
놀라운 원동력은
어디서 나오나
기적을 일으키는
절대 침묵 속이리
"그러니 너희는 진정하여라"*
바다가 갈라지며
길이 드러나는 걸 보게 되리
*출애굽기 14:14

River of Tears

The world without gratitude

And with moving muted;

What tears?

A soft spring rain on the frozen soil

To sprout new shoots.

Either tears of victory

Or those of defeat

Are the gift from Heaven

By tugging at our heartstrings loud

To awaken the sleeping soul.

The world of indignation and confrontation,

Cruelty and cold-heartedness;

The day a sentiment of sympathies surges up

Tears that fill the heart

Will form a river overflowing.

눈물의 강

감사가 없고
감동이 사라진 세상
어찌된 눈물인가
언 땅에 봄비를 내려
새싹을 돋아 내려서리

승리의 눈물이나
패배의 눈물이나
하늘의 선물이리
심금을 크게 울려
잠든 영혼을 깨우리

분노와 대결
잔인과 학대의 세상
가슴을 적시던 눈물이
연민의 정이 복받치는 날
넘쳐흐르는 강을 이루리

October Wind

Brilliant beams of sunlight

Riding on an October wind

Pour down over the dancing forest.

As rapture is won in the aspiration,

Joyful shouts rock the whole world.

Now that love defeats all,

Liberty will run over in peace.

Just beholding

Leads joys to brim over.

With hair blowing,

A sublime poise is approaching.

Thinking only

Makes me full of love,

A fair face smiling.

Stunning colors

Carried on an October wind

Crowd into the heart.

As holding the grace within the hope,

We will not fear even with night falling.

Having received all through prayers,

We will live in peace and freedom.

시월 바람

눈부신 빛살이
시월 바람을 타고
춤추는 숲으로 쏟아진다
열망 가운데 환희를 얻었으니
기쁨의 함성이 천지를 흔든다
사랑으로 모두를 이겼기에
평화 안에 자유가 넘치지

바라만 보아도
기쁨이 넘쳐흐르지
머리카락 날리며
다가오는 숭고한 자태
생각만 해도
사랑이 벅차오르지
미소 짓는 아름다운 얼굴

놀라운 색깔들이
시월 바람에 실려
가슴 안으로 밀려든다
소망 가운데 은혜를 잡았으니
저무는 날에도 두렵지 않지
기원으로 모두를 받았기에
평화와 자유 안에 살아가지

Restoring Order

If the destruction of order is a disease,
Good health means a cultivation of order.
Healing is a recuperating process
Back to the original order.

In the universe of order and chaos,
Hurt and healing live together.
Even parts are swinging by chaos,
The whole is controlled by order.

We may be swayed for a moment by chaos,
Finally we will live in order.
Seemingly we may collapse by disease
In fact, it is the process of restoring order.

질서 회복

질서의 붕괴가 병이라면
건강은 질서의 함양이리
치유는 본시의 질서로
돌아가는 회복의 과정

질서와 혼란의 우주에서
상처와 치유가 함께 산다
부분은 혼돈에 흔들리나
전체는 질서가 다스리지

잠시는 혼돈에 흔들리나
결국엔 질서 안에서 살지
겉보기는 병으로 무너지나
실은 질서 회복의 과정이지

The Upheaval of the World

The gap between smile and indignation,

Welcome and refusal,

And delight and pathos,

Looks deep and deep.

But the day the abyss turns into the plain,

The paradise will be created.

On an intersection of emotions,

A circuit of memory,

And the transcendental network,

Marvelous flames spout out

To overthrow the world.

Down from the loftiest spot,

The signal of the upheaval of the world

Sets a big fire on the central nerve

That spreads through synapse.

The fall deep into the abyss

Will soar up to the zenith.

개벽

미소와 분노 사이
환영과 거절 사이
환희와 비애 사이
천길만길 같지만
나락이 개벽되면
천국을 이루게 되리

감성의 교차로
기억의 회로
초월적 네트워크에
놀라운 불길이 확 치솟아
천지가 뒤집히지

지극히 높은 데서
내려오는 개벽 신호가
중추에 큰 불길을 올려
시냅스를 타고 퍼져 가리
심연으로 내닫던 추락이
천정을 향하여 비상하지

After Loss

Possessed by loud applause,

I lost delicate tremors.

Running for quite a while,

I find myself taking the course against the sun.

To wrap up the wound I made,

I wander for the whole life of mine.

Having received and won

Great and many things

As a matter of course,

How can I perceive all?

After loss,

I barely notice something missing.

잃은 다음

요란한 갈채에 홀려
미세한 울림을 놓치고
한참 달리다 보면
빛을 등지고 달리지
제가 입힌 상처를 싸매려
한평생을 쏘다니리

크고 많은 걸
붙박이로
받고 얻었기에
어찌 다 감지하랴
잃은 다음에야 겨우
빠진 걸 알아차리지

Footsteps

Amid the fallen leaves swept away,
The autumn's back is seen to leave.
In the midst of rainstorm, with big strides,
Approaching footsteps of early winter are heard.

The fragrance of wild flowers covering the fields
And sociable smiles and whispers as well,
Carried on the river running leisurely,
Will arrive at the sea turning around the estuary.

The space vacated by wind and rain,
What will come and fill out?
Now an act will soon be done,
The next will prepare for a new meeting.

How does time run idly?
Sometime, for some reason and cause,
The voyage was occultly designed,
The way contains a great will.

발소리

날려 가는 낙엽들 속으로
떠나가는 가을의 뒷모습
비바람 가운데 성큼성큼
다가오는 초겨울 발소리

벌판을 덮던 들꽃 향기도
다정한 미소도 속삭임도
유유히 흐르는 강에 실려
강어귀를 돌아 바다에 닿지

비바람이 비워 놓은 자리는
무엇이 들어와 채워 주려나
한 막이 이제 곧 끝나리니
새 만남을 다음이 준비하지

시간이 어찌 헛되이 달리리
언젠가 왜인지 어째서인지
오묘하게 설계된 항해이기에
그 길엔 큰 뜻이 담겨 있으리

Debris

Behind the wings of pompous power,

In the procession of radiant riches,

Darkness spreads and seeps through unknowingly.

A bitter feeling is hard to cast off

As debris of worldly honors lingers.

Till when do you remain a prisoner

Of passing earthly prosperity.?

To what time do you repeat

Self-deception?

Endlessly questioning sound

Will be heard from the deep inside.

Debris of constellations is blown by a blast,

Its scattering din resonates over the horizon,

As if asking us to listen to

And raise our eyes to look over

The signal letting us find shelter.

잔해

장려한 권좌의 날개 뒤로
눈부신 부귀의 행렬 안에
어느새 깔려 들어오는 어둠
떨칠 수 없는 쓸쓸한 느낌
영화의 잔해가 어른거려서리

언제까지 스쳐 갈 영화의
포로가 될 건가
자기기만을 어디까지
되풀이할 건가
깊은 데서 끊임없이
묻는 소리 들려오리

성좌의 잔해가 폭풍에 날린다
흩어지는 소리 지평을 울린다
귀 기울여 들어보라는 거리
눈 들어 넘어다보라는 거리
피난처를 알려주는 신호이리

Verticality and Horizontality

Heaven and I,

Heaven and you,

The vertical relation should be right,

Then you and I

The horizontal relation follows

To start and develop.

Not once

But the task of everyday and every hour;

A succession of strenuous selections

And endless struggles.

All overcome,

A wondrous day will come

When the vertical and the horizon

Gather together.

Heaven descends to the earth

To brighten the earth like Heaven.

수직과 수평

하늘과 나
하늘과 너
수직관계가 바로 서야
너와 나
수평관계가 따라서
시작되고 발전하리

한 번이 아니라
매일 매시의 과제이지
피나는 선택의 연속
끝없는 싸움이리

모두가 극복되고
수직과 수평이
함께 모이는
놀라운 날이 오리니
하늘이 땅에 내려와
땅을 하늘같이 빛내리

Quintet

Tunes tugged by heart,
Reverberation struck by soul
Tap remote hills infinitely
And flutter to reach the zenith.

They raise by playing
To soar up to the sky
And tug and tap
To reach the other side.

It will soothe the swaying minds
And encourage struggling souls.
Footsteps of aspiration running,
A quintet is completing the whole.

오중주

마음이 짜내는 선율
영혼이 퉁기는 울림
먼 산을 한없이 두드린다
천정에 닿으려 날개 친다

켜서 올린다
하늘로 솟으려
뜯고 두드린다
너머에 닿으려

흔들리는 마음 가다듬는다
몸부림치는 영혼 북돋워 주리
열망이 달려가는 발소리
온전을 이루어 가는 오중주

Respiration and Palpitation

All the world is respiration and palpitation,

Inhales life and

Exhales death

To circulate vitality all over the body

In order to survive for good and all.

Minute particles, molecules and cells

After catching their breath,

To the pulse

By beating their feet

To where they live,

Swim without rest.

You and I, we all

Climbing and crossing over the waves

Feel breathless with the heart moving.

As respiration controls our heart,

So palpitation rules over our thought.

호흡과 박동

세상 모두는 호흡과 박동
삶을 빨아들이고
죽음을 내뱉으며
생기를 혼신에 돌려댄다
언제까지나 살고 싶어서리

미립자 분자 세포들
호흡을 가다듬고
박동에 맞추어
발장구치며
살 곳을 향해
쉬지 않고 헤엄친다

너와 나 우리 전부
파도를 오르고 넘느라
숨차고 가슴 설레지
호흡이 마음을 조절하니
박동은 생각을 다스리지

Discernment

The universe of light and dark,

The world of joys and sorrows,

Not knowing the direction of proceeding,

We just tremble with fear.

The way of creation and extinction,

The mind of love and agony,

Not knowing the reason of making,

We only wail in grief.

To pave the road to discernment,

Let us cry out in tears.

To learn the way to win,

Let our heartstrings tugged at.

분별

빛과 어둠의 우주
기쁨과 슬픔의 세상
어디론지도 모르며
무서워 떨지

생성과 소멸의 길
사랑과 고뇌의 마음
어째선지도 모르며
슬피 우는가

분별의 길을 닦게
울고 불게 하리
이기는 길을 알게
심금을 울려 주리

Grand Finale

Listen carefully.

Amid the gorgeous sunset glow,

An aubade greeting the dawn will be heard.

Look into attentively.

Riding the resonation of a grand finale,

A panorama of the other side will be revealed.

대단원

귀를 기울여 들어라
놀라운 낙조 가운데서
여명의 노래가 들려오리

유심히 들여다보아라
대단원의 울림을 타고
너머의 전경이 드러나리

Part 5

Focal Point

초점

Focal Point

By aiming at the focal point right

I will grasp the beginning,

Then be invited to an amazing nation

Where only the never-ending beginning exists.

On the marvelous revolving stage,

The focal point is swallowed into the end,

Then I will be entangled

In an unbearably frightful chain of chaos.

The curtain drops on the stage.

The actor focusing on the next,

After changing the old suit into a new one,

Will emerge again in a burst of applause.

초점

초점을 바로 맞춰
시작을 붙잡아야지
끝없이 처음만 있는
놀라운 나라에 초대되지

경이로운 회전무대에서
초점이 끝자락에 휘말리면
견딜 수 없이 두려운
혼돈의 사슬에 얽히지

무대에 막이 내려진다
다음에 초점을 모은 배우
낡은 옷 새로 갈아입고
갈채 속에 다시 등장하지

Flames

Weaving moments of truth

To cherish in eternity,

Blazing flames

Planted from time immemorial.

To see what is unseen,

A shout entreats eagerly.

Plowing through the mist of doubt,

A face thinks in agony

Sometime with a good news,

A jubilant look will beam.

Fervent flares

Will catch up the target.

At last we will receive

What is impossible.

불길

진실의 순간을 엮어
영원에 간직하려나
태초에 깊이 심어 준
타오르는 불길

안 보이는 걸 보게
간구하는 외침
의심의 안개를 헤치며
고뇌하는 얼굴
언젠간 기쁜 소식에
환희의 눈빛 빛나리

간절한 불길이니
표적을 잡게 되리
불가능하던 걸
드디어 받게 되리

December Fog

Trees submerged in December fog
Stand dreary on the horizon.
Into the dim sky,
A flock of birds fly.
For what reason and what to do,
Nobody says anything
Deep down waiting for something.

You and I, the flight of birds,
Beholding leaf shoots,
Awaiting floral buds,
All, shoving along the fog,
Will run to the site
Where the sun shines.

Following the beam of light,
We'll reach the source.
Before dropping down,
New sprouts have already been prepared.
To the brightly sparkling eyes,
Lush leaves already dance
And fluorescent flowers sing.

섣달 안개

섣달 안개에 잠긴 나무들이
을씨년스레 지평에 늘어섰다
어렴풋한 하늘 속으로
어째선지 무얼 하려는지
새무리들이 날아간다
아무도 아무 말 안 하나
무언갈 기다리는 눈치다

너와 나 새떼들
바라보는 잎눈들
기다리는 꽃망울들
모두가 안개를 헤치며
빛이 스며드는 쪽
거기를 향해 달려가지

빛을 따라가다 보면
원천에 이르게 되리
떨어지기 전에 이미
새 돋음이 준비되리니
밝게 빛나는 눈엔 벌써
무성한 잎들이 춤추지
화사한 꽃들이 노래하지

Groups of the Moment

Here is just
The fleeting port of call
Where groups of the moment grope the beyond
And glance around to be tightly embraced.

Shouts out of life are mingled with wind waves;
Joy and sorrow sing and dance.
When waves on the flow break against the cliff,
The moment weaves patterns with traces.

Right at this site,
Sent from somewhere,
Groups of the moment endlessly
Tap the gate of eternity.

순간의 무리들

이곳이 바로
순간의 무리들이 너머를 더듬고
깊이 안기고 싶어 두리번거리는
덧없는 기항지이지

삶의 외침이 풍랑에 섞이는데
기쁨과 슬픔이 노래하며 춤추지
밀려온 파도가 절벽에 부서질 때
순간은 흔적을 모아 무늬를 짜지

바로 여기서
어디선가 보내온
순간의 무리들이 끝없이
영원의 문을 두드리지

A Flowering Tree

After planting a flowering tree,
The expecting mind
Sees flower buds.
When wind blows, rain drops,
Then rain passes flowers bloom.
I will run grasping this promise.

Rainfall has already gone.
But because of an overcast sky,
A cozy spring tide to burst out
Hard bud shells is remote.
Signals are frequent,
Florescence, however, is so tardy.

The mind growing a flowering tree is
To bloom distant tomorrows.
What flowers to be open,
What are these blossoms to do,
Where do these flowers stand
And who are waiting for them?

꽃나무

꽃나무를 심어 놓고
고대하는 마음에
꽃망울이 섰다
바람이 불면 비가 오고
비가 스치면 꽃이 핀다니
이 약속 붙들고 달려가리

빗발은 이미 지나갔는데
구름이 하늘을 덮쳐선가
단단한 눈까풀 터뜨려 줄
포근한 빛 소식은 아득하다
신호는 자주 보내오는데
어찌 개화는 이리 더딘가

꽃나무를 가꾸는 뜻은
먼 내일을 피우려서지
어떤 꽃을 피어 낼지
무엇 할 꽃이 피어날지
어디에 설 꽃이 될지
누가 기다리는 꽃일지

Not the End

Even being dispersed
And disappeared,
That is not the end.

Passing the afterglow
And crossing the margin,
I will start again.
Despite being unseen
And unheard of,
I will live there.

A new appearance
And new vigor
Makes me survive.

끝이 아니지

흩어져도
사라져도
끝이 아니지

여운을 지나
여백을 넘어
다시 시작하지
안 보여도
안 들려도
거기서 살지

새 모습으로
새 기운으로
다시 살아가지

Songs without Words

My beloved!

What song are you preparing for?

Is it the vibration of birds

Waiting for the morning

In the forest at dead night?

Or is it the whisper of leaf buds

Responding with smile

To the approaching sunshine?

Songs of evening dews dangling from petals,

Moans of fallen leaves scattering about the road,

And reverberations of light rays in tune with darkness.

Who creates like that and for what?

My beloved!

What song do you sing?

The choir of the galaxies

Covering the horizon of deep space,

What does it inform of?

Songs without words of minute particles

Drawing dazzling orbits,

What do they signify?

무언가 無言歌

사랑하는 이여
무슨 노래를 준비하나요
아침을 기다리는
깊은 밤 숲속
새들의 떨림인가요
다가오는 빛살에
미소 지어 답하는
잎눈들의 속삭임인가요

꽃잎에 맺힌 저녁이슬의 노래
가로에 흩어지는 낙엽들의 신음
어둠을 안고 율동하는 빛살의 울림은
누가 왜 그렇게 지어내나요

사랑하는 이여
무슨 노래를 들려주려나요
심우주의 지평을 덮는
은하들의 합창은
무엇을 알리려 하나요
눈부신 궤도를 그려 가는
미립자들의 무언가는
무슨 의미인가요

Prayers to Hear

As the vocal cords are so much raised,

Minute whispers

Are too swept by voices

To be heard.

As flaming shouts

And entreating wails

Are so great and intense,

The response is muted.

Prayers are covert dialogues,

Each other's intimate communications.

Earnest appeals are significant

But attentive listening is more valuable.

In absolute silence

Replies are always awaiting.

Let those able to hear listen

Prayers to hear lead to close listening

듣는 기도

목청이 너무 컸기에
목소리에 묻혀
미세한 음성이
들리지 않았지
열망의 불길 소리가
간구의 울부짖음이
너무나 크고 강렬해
응답이 가려졌지

기도는 은밀한 대화
서로의 긴밀한 교제
간청도 중요하나
경청이 더욱 값지지
절대 침묵 가운데서
음성은 언제나 기다리지
들을 수 있는 이 듣게 되리
듣는 기도가 듣게 해 주리

Immortal Tomorrow

In the drizzling hospital front yard,

Lilacs bloomed in various colors

Are blown top and tail by wind.

Welcome or farewell, ambiguous.

Either glad dance or awkward gesture,

The eyes looking up will decide.

Who they are visiting or have visited

And what they have heard or are going to hear of?

A myriad of faces comes in and out of the entrance.

"At this age that is enough."

"Why such a thing happens at that age?"

"As there is no improvement, he is ready to accept now."

Always even amid black clouds,

Anywhere in rainstorms,

Flowers bloom in our garden.

Not sobbing and wailing at situations

But trusting everything to the immortal tomorrow,

We won't lament over today's darkness.

불후의 내일

병원 앞 정원 부슬비 속에
여러 빛깔로 핀 라일락 무리
머리와 사지가 바람에 날린다
환영인지 환송인지 애매하다
기쁜 춤인지 버거운 몸짓인지
바라보는 시각이 결정해 주리

누구를 보러 오는지 보고 가는지
무얼 듣고 가는지 들으러 오는지
수많은 얼굴이 현관을 드나든다
"이 나이에 이만하면 되었지"
"그 나이에 어찌 그런 일이 생기나"
"차도가 없으니 이제 각오하라나 봐"

먹구름 가운데서도 언제나
비바람 속에서도 어디서나
우리의 정원에는 꽃이 피어나지
상황에 무너져 울고 불지 않고
불후의 내일에 모두를 맡겼기에
오늘이 어둡다고 한탄하지 않지

Free Will

As there is an elaborate shape

And esoteric order,

They fly freely in the space

With fiery wings fixed.

Not locked in,

Nor confined,

But to spread out our free will,

Time and space has been opened.

Not to flee by stirring

The harmony of amazing order,

But try to grasp something more valuable

Existing higher and deeper.

Only within the sublime order,

The exquisite life will be sustained.

Between temptation and vocation,

There will be the choice of free will.

자유의지

정교한 형상과
신묘한 질서가 있기에
불 날개를 달고
우주를 종횡하지 않느냐

갇혀 있지 않게
매어 살지 않게
자유의지를 펼치게
시공을 열어 주었지

놀라운 질서의 조화를
휘젓고 도망치는 게 아니지
더 높이 더 깊이 있을
더 귀중한 걸 잡아 보라는 거리

숭고한 질서 안에서만
절묘한 삶은 유지되지
유혹과 부름 사이에
자유의지의 선택이 있지

Penumbra

Amid calling and temptation,

Around the boundary between light and dark,

We live amid penumbra

Dim as life and dream mingled up.

To learn wisdom of distinguishing

Truth and falsehood,

We are trained within.

Between hope and desire,

Border of beasts and humans,

Between mortals and immortals,

We struggle amid penumbra

To get rid of dirt

And to be perfect

While passing the dusk.

반영 半影

부름과 유혹 사이
빛과 어둠의 경계
삶과 꿈이 섞여 흐릿한
반영 가운데서 살아가지
진실과 거짓을
분별할 지혜를 익히려
그 안에서 길들이는 거리

소망과 욕구 사이
짐승과 사람의 경계
사람과 신 사이
반영 가운데서 허덕이지
어스름 속을 지나는 동안
때를 벗겨 내라는 거리
온전히 되어 보라는 거리

Relay Race

On the site floral waves have flowed,

Light green seawater surges.

In an empty nest with petals blown out,

Tomorrow seeds are ripening

By grasping a relay baton.

To seize the day,

Yesterday have crossed

And today will cross the finish line,

By handing over a relay baton.

To catch the light,

Today and tomorrow

Have risen and will rise again

Running a relay race.

Into the rain down with melodies,

The wind slides to the tune.

Leaves and twigs swaying in the wood,

All give and take the baton;

The world is all a relay race.

릴레이 경주

꽃물결이 흘러간 자리로
연초록 바다가 밀려든다
꽃잎이 날려 간 빈 둥지에서
릴레이 바통을 벌써 움켜쥔
내일의 씨가 여물어 가지

한때를 잡으려
바통을 주고받으며
어제가 결승선을 건넜고
오늘이 또 건너지
빛을 잡으려
오늘과 내일이
릴레이하며
오르고 또 오르지

가락을 타고 내리는 빗속으로
장단 맞추어 미끄러지는 바람
흔들리는 숲의 잎과 가지들
모두 바통을 주고받는다
세상이 모두 릴레이 경주다

Sand Painting

The wind on the sands

Is beginning to draw a picture

To leave some traces

As its share.

What is your pipe depicting?

Who is your keyboard calling for?

To paint its share dark,

The heartbeat never cease for a moment.

To carve traces deep,

Breaths always huff and puff.

Even traces are vanishing

And shares are being forgotten,

I tug the strings

And you tap the drum.

Not seen but recorded somewhere.

Not heard but somebody remembers.

모래 그림

바람이 모래 위에
그림을 그려 간다
흔적을 내 두려
몫으로 알고
너의 피리는 무엇을 그려 가나
나의 건반은 누구를 부르는가

몫을 진하게 칠하려
박동은 잠시도 그치지 않지
흔적을 깊이 새기려
숨소리는 늘 헐떡거리지

흔적이 사라져 가도
몫이 묻혀 잊혀져도
나는 현을 퉁기지
너는 북을 울리리
보이지 않아도 어딘가에 기록되지
들리지 않아도 누군가는 기억하리

Mysteries

To spread out mysteries,

Time has to run an endless marathon,

Cosmos expands restlessly.

To bloom pretty without growing old,

Quarks* making up protons

Sing and dance in rainbow-stripped garments

Choked with longing,

The lung always gasps

And the heart throbs all the time.

A masterpiece ready to be born to shake our souls,

Flames are blazing in the heart,

Storms striking in the brain.

They are put on board the mysterious wings

To penetrate the black hole

Into the way to an eternal rest.

*elementary particles supposed to make up protons and
neutrons.

불가사의

불가사의를 펼쳐 내려
시간은 끊임없이 달려야 하지
우주는 쉬지 않고 팽창해야지
늙지 않고 늘 곱게 피어나려
양자 안의 쿼크*들은
색동옷 입고 춤추며 노래하지

그리움이 가슴을 메어
허파는 늘 허덕여야 하지
심장은 언제나 설레야 하리

영혼을 흔드는 걸작이 태어나려
가슴에는 불길이 타올라야 하지
머리에는 폭풍이 불어쳐야 하리
불가사의한 날개에 태운다
블랙홀을 뚫고 나가보란다
영원한 안식에 드는 길이리

*양자를 구성하는 소립자

Expression and Subject

Expressions are different,

But subjects the same.

Songs of the stars and dances of minute particles;

The heart-striking wind and the space-shaking lightning
bolt;

Upon the occult main melodies of genes,

Amazing variations of the soul are blooming!

Appearances are different

But contents the same.

Love millennial years ago and Longing ten thousand years
later;

Breath rising and falling and footsteps coming and going;

From the subject of awesome light dances,

What a splendid variation of the mind arises!

표현과 주제

표현은 다르나
주제는 같지
별들의 노래 소립자의 무도
가슴에 치는 바람 우주를 흔드는 섬광
유전자의 신묘한 주 선율에서
영혼의 놀라운 변주가 피다니

모습은 다르나
내용은 같지
천년 전 사랑 만년 후 동경
피고 지는 숨소리 오가는 발소리
경이로운 빛 춤의 주제에서
마음의 장려한 변주가 일다니

Future

Our future is

A journey of zeal

Running toward the beginning.

The original starting point is

A fantastic hometown

Engraved in the longing.

On the road blooming and fading,

On the stage pushed and pulled,

We will hold a ball

Wearing a host of masks.

Future is the way home

To reach the site dreamed of.

Not only do merry plays appear

But also bloody games.

Tears are not always sorrowful

And songs are not mirthful all the time.

미래

우리의 미래는
시작으로 달려가는
열망의 여정
시작의 원점은
동경 안에 새겨진
환상적 고향

피고 지는 행로 위
밀고 밀리는 무대에서
무수한 탈을 쓰고
무도회를 열어 가리

미래는 고향으로 가는 길
꿈꾸던 곳에 이르게 되리
어찌 기쁜 놀이만 있으랴
피 흘리는 게임도 있지
눈물이 어찌 다 슬프랴
노래가 어찌 다 기쁘랴

Windmill

Windmill

Infinitely turning and turning,

Does it scoop up

Or pour down?

Time

Restlessly running,

Gathers to pile up

Or breaks to scatter over.

It looks it's going to break,

But it is rebuilding.

It seems to be thrown away,

But it is to be reaped.

풍차

한없이
돌아가는 풍차
퍼 담으려나
쏟아 버리려나

쉬지 않고
달려가는 시간
모아 세우기도 하고
부수어 흩기도 하지

부수는 것 같으나
다시 세우는 거리
버려지는 듯싶으나
다시 거둬지는 거지